D0771355

What Children Tell Me about Angels

What Children Tell Me about Angels

Charlie W. Shedd

Servant Publications
Ann Arbor, Michigan

Vine Books is an imprint of Servant Publications especially designed to serve evangelical Christians.

All the names and other identifying details contained in these stories have been changed to protect the privacy of those involved. Some of these stories are composites of the experiences of several people, as the author recalls them.

Published by Servant Publications
P.O. Box 8617
Ann Arbor, Michigan 48107

Cover design by Multnomah Graphics
Cover illustration by Miles Pinckney
Interior illustrations by Patrick J. Powers

95 96 97 98 99 10 9 8 7 6 5 4 3 2

Printed in the United States of America
ISBN 0-89283-901-5

Library of Congress Cataloging-in-Publication Data

Shedd, Charlie W.
What children tell me about angels / Charlie W. Shedd.
p. cm.
ISBN 0-89283-901-5
1. Angels. 2. Children—Religious life. 3. Christian life.
I. Title.
BT966.2.S533 1995
235'.3—dc20 95-6837
CIP

Contents

Part IV THREE STORIES FROM A NORTHERN LAKE

Part V ANGELS TO THE RESCUE

Part VI LESSONS FROM THE ANGELS

Part VII ANGELS AND THE ANIMALS

Part VIII TRAFFIC WAYS FOR ANGELS

Let's Start Right Here

Does the Lord have an entire retinue of angels who work especially with children? Most parents, grandparents, and teachers wouldn't find this hard to believe. As children think their pensive thoughts about earth, heaven and angels, where do these thoughts originate? Are they from a source we've lost touch with in our adulthood? If we must say "Yes" to this question, then how's this for an addition to our prayer life?

Lord, thank you for the fresh
breezes from children
blessing the barren places of our
so-called "grown-upness."

The Bible tells us we "are a little lower than the angels" (Hebrews 2:7). Yet the same Bible makes it clear that human beings can be God's traffic ways. And that includes children of any age in many places. I know because I'm often invited to all kinds of interface with the young. From coast to coast I've interviewed Sunday school classes, youth clubs, Christian schools and secular. Everywhere, the welcome rug is out. Come, Grandpa, let's probe the angel theme together. Enthusiasm plus. Wisdom plus.

Then there are two other sources opening windows through which I see more angels doing their thing. One source is the flood of letters coming as a response to my simple request in *Brush of an Angel's Wing*. From places near and far numerous correspondents go back in their personal history to give me their input—accounts of amazing experiences from their childhood. Angel touches in their childhood.

Yet that's not all. From deep inside me many almost forgotten memories have surfaced, witnessing to the reality of angels. I hope as you near the age of eighty this wonderful thing will happen to you as it has to me—you will be able to remember far far back in your own days gone by. Long forgotten events, here they come. The time your phone rang and it changed your life. A stranger knocked at your door with that happy surprise. From out of nowhere came welcome positives, downers that later turned to uppers, or mysteries still unsolved.

Don't hurry it. The years are going to pass anyway, but one day you will be able to say with me this credo from *Brush of an Angel's Wing:*

I believe in a loving God
whose angels are never far away.
Therefore, even when things seem to the contrary
I believe that his universe and my life in it
are unfolding as they should
and everything is on schedule.

MEET JARRETT, MY GRANDSON AND CHILD CONSULTANT

Is there any grandfather who doesn't think his grandchildren are the smartest ever?

Not this one!

Jarrett is eight. He is good-looking, full of fun, accommodating, and an avid reader. He's also a champion gymnast. When I began *What Children Tell Me about Angels,* it was obvious I'd soon need special help.

So, throughout this book, I will share with you the cool wisdom of my favorite (and only) grandson. My exchanges with Jarrett may be found in the sections of this book called "Except Ye Become as Little Children...." After reading Jarrett's comments, my editor agreed that this eight-year-old has a special handle on the world of angels.

I know that you will think so, too.

HOW TO USE THIS BOOK

The stories told here have been tested for usability. Parents have found them helpful in family devotions, at discussion times around the dinner table, for goodnight thinking, too. Teachers in Sunday schools, public schools, Christian schools, and one special education school for the mentally handicapped have used them also. But I especially like it when grandparents report sharing angel thoughts with their favorite people.

That Sign DID Read "Toad Road"

Part One

What Else Could It Be But Angels?

Four boys equal eight eyes, don't they? How could eight eyes see the same sign where there wasn't any sign? And could a swimming pool ball get up by itself and walk? How could it move to the exact spot where a tiny tot would fall?

How could the lives of two championship basketball players be united one day in the heart of a little girl? And out there on a remote field, how could two men in white lift a tractor and go away with no comment?

Where do such dashes of wonder originate? Whose *are* these unseen hands? What else could it be but angels?

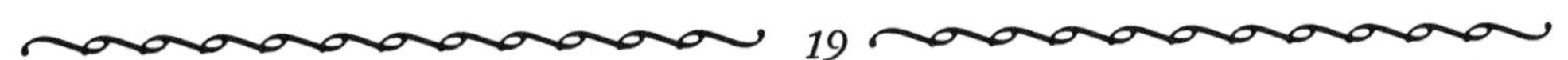

That Sign DID Read "Toad Road"

Catfish Reed was his name. He was not exactly every parent's idea of the perfect river buddy for their junior-high son. Catfish was tall. He was thin. He didn't have a regular job. He was also missing one front tooth. This meant he wasn't exactly tidy. Why? Because Catfish chewed tobacco, spitting often, and his aim was undependable.

For all these reasons the adult world did not care much for Catfish. But to his river buddies, he was a hero. He knew where the catfish were, and he told us. That made a big difference. We spent much time at the river and we were big on catfish cookouts.

We also liked to win rowboat races. Every year on our Cedar River there were many races. Up river, down river, across river, winning for us was a cinch. Why? Because Catfish knew where the rocks were and he would chart our course to perfection. Let others smash up, slow up, give up. Not us. With Catfish on shore waving us here, there, off to the right, off to the left, no question. Give us the trophy and you go for second.

Then, one summer morning Catfish wasn't there. Which, for him, was a never-never. A.M., P.M., any time, any day, the river and Catfish flowed together. So up and down river we went, asking, "Has anyone seen Catfish?"

"Nope. Ain't seen him no where. Mighta' died. We all gonna go sometime, ya know."

So into the pickup we piled ourselves and off we started. None of us had ever been to his home. All we knew was that he had said he lived on "Toad Road. Way back toward the swamp. Mile maybe."

Off the main river road there were countless little roads, lanes, paths taking off to who knew where. One of these had to be "Toad Road," but which one? Our only clue was one other thing Catfish once told us: "'bout one car wide."

So off we went up and down looking for "Toad Road" one car wide. We found too many lanes matching that description. But if our buddy needed us, we must find him.

Whatever could we do?

Now I am about to tell you something you will hardly believe. But please don't go away. On one of those many trips up and down the river road with its numerous cut-offs, a miracle happened.

Suddenly out of nowhere we spotted a sign, a weatherbeaten old board with the words, "Toad Road." The two in front spied it first. Peeling white letters on an old brown board. Then the two of us in back saw it, too. Clear.

You will know we wasted no time getting to that shack Catfish called home. There we found him sick, very sick. Quickly we did what you'd have done. Putting a worn old mattress and some blankets in our pickup, off we went to the hospital.

"Just in time, boys," the doctor said. "This man is in a bad way."

From that moment on it was the best of attention for Catfish. Reason? Good little hospital and, as a side factor, the doctor's son had grown up on our river. Fact is, his was the frumpy old pickup we'd used to look for our hero.

Gradually Catfish recovered. He returned to his tobacco-chewing self. And we were, to borrow a phrase from Scripture, "filled with joy and gladness."

Then one day when we were hanging around his hospital room we told him about our hunt for "Toad Road."

"Almost missed that sign, Catfish. Ought to get you a new sign."

"The sign you got is getting old. Barely read the letters."

"What sign you talkin' 'bout? They ain't no sign there. Never has been. Never."

We went back to get it to show Catfish. But he was right. No "Toad Road" sign. Hardly a day of his recovery went on when we would not harangue loud and long about that sign.

"Couldn't have been."

"Oh, yes, it was."

"You guys been seein' things."

"Honest, Catfish, it was there. I saw it with my own two eyes. All four of us saw it. No way we could miss it. 'Toad Road.'"

"Well, I'm tellin' you somethin', men. (Another reason we liked him—sometimes he called us "men.") That name 'Toad Road' was a name I give it. Sort of a joke, you know? That road's so hidden it don't have a real name."

"Except Ye Become as Little Children . . ."

Grandpa: *"What do you think happened, Jarrett? All four of us saw the sign. When we looked for it again, where did it go?"*

Jarrett: *"That's easy, Grandpa. An angel came and held up the sign so you would know this was Toad Road. Then the angel went back to heaven with the sign."*

Grandpa: *"But, Jarrett, why didn't we see the angel?"*

Jarrett: *"Grandpa, you weren't LOOKING for an angel."*

Question for pondering:

Would we see more angels
if we were looking
for them more?

24

Who Moved the Swimming Pool Ball?

The drop was sixteen feet from the upstairs porch to the game room basement door. And that is some fall for a twenty-seven-month-old boy. But that's how far he fell—from the upstairs porch to a solid cement platform at the game room entrance.

His name was Brandon, which is somewhat chic for a boy into everything like he was.

His parents were taking their Sunday afternoon nap in the upstairs bedroom. Brandon was napping in his crib at the foot of their bed. But Brandon woke early. What a good time to explore the upstairs bedroom porch. Nice porch. Nice flowers. Nice view. Nice for a twenty-seven-month-old to be feeling so high up.

Being Brandon, he explored the porch thoroughly. He plucked some of his mother's flowers and examined the cast-iron fence. He viewed the yard through its bars. But wouldn't his world look even more interesting if he could sit on the fence top and ponder it from there?

So, being Brandon, he climbed to the top. Now swing the feet, view the view, wave to anyone needing a wave.

This fun finished, Brandon asked himself, "How do I get down from here? Think. Turn around, Brandon, very slowly. Put your feet over the other side and very, very slowly go back the way you came."

Only, in turning around, his foot slipped and suddenly he was going down another way. Straight down. Down to the concrete below.

Boom, he landed. Only, praises be, not on the cement landing, but straight in the middle of the swimming pool ball. Soft, bouncy, sort of fun really.

From that day on, for a long time there was almost no other conversation around the family table than this: *Who moved the swimming pool ball?* Who put it right there in the very spot where Brandon would fall? Nobody ever carried that ball anywhere. Too big and awkward. The older kids with their friends wouldn't have moved it. Too lazy. Mother didn't move it. Dad didn't. Neighbors didn't. So who moved it?

All over town, the club, bridge meetings, office coffee breaks. Everywhere the same question, same answer. Nobody had the faintest idea. Nobody except Brandon's father. Being the pastor of a fast-growing congregation, he preached some sermons on "Miracles of the Bible." Great series, real provocative, but as he himself said, "Surprising how many miracles are shrouded in permanent mystery. Let's sing again the chorus from that old favorite, 'Angels Watching over Me.'"

"Except Ye Become as Little Children . . ."

Grandpa: *"However did the swimming pool ball get to the exact spot where a little boy would fall?"*

Jarrett: *"An angel put it there. It was too bulky for anyone else to move. I've been in lots of pools with balls like that."* (Jarrett is an excellent swimmer.) *"Only an angel would be strong enough to move it so fast."*

Grandpa: *"Do you think the angel saw the little boy fall and then moved it?"*

Jarrett: *"Sure."*

Grandpa: *"But how could he move it that fast if it was all that heavy?"*

Jarrett: *"Grandpa, don't you know angels are like Superman? They can lift anything. They can move faster than the speed of light."*

Grandpa: *"Well then, when the angel saw the boy sitting on the rail, why didn't he pick him up and put him where he belonged? Wouldn't that make more sense?"*

Jarrett: *"No, he had to teach the parents a lesson."*

Grandpa: *"A lesson? What lesson?"*

Jarrett: *"The lesson is that parents shouldn't keep dangerous doors unlocked when they have little boys."*

The Bible says,

"Out of the mouths
of babes..."

Matthew 21:16

"My Mother Married the Dentist"

My mother and I moved to this big city over two years ago when my father died. My grandparents live here and they wanted us to be near them. Since my mother is a nurse she can get a job almost anywhere.

Well, I got this awful toothache before we found a dentist here, so my mother looked up "dentist" in the yellow pages. She ran her finger down the list until she came to a Dr. Brown. That was the same last name as our best friends back home. So we went to him and he was nice. He gave me some stuff to make my tooth quit hurting. Then he fixed it so it wouldn't hurt anymore.

While he was fixing my tooth he asked about my name. Some people think it is a funny name, with twelve letters and only three of them vowels. I guess it is, but I have had it so long it doesn't sound strange to me. Well, hardly anybody has ever heard of it but the dentist had. He said he played basketball in high school with a boy who had that name. Then he asked my father's name. Archie was my father's name and he played basketball, too. I told him a picture of Dad's team hangs in our hall. Before he died my father loved to tell about being conference champions. I missed my dad a lot. Dr. Brown told me he knew how we must have felt when dad died because his wife died last year.

Then Dr. Brown got a curious look on his face, and he asked me my mother's first name. I told him "Louise." Right then he stopped what he was doing and asked me if my father had red hair and my mother had blond. I nodded. He said my mother was two grades behind my dad and him. They had all gone to high school together. He didn't know her very well because she was younger, but he heard she was a very nice girl. I told him she was still nice, usually. So he asked if it would be OK if he called. I said, "Yes," and he did that very night. Well, they talked a long time and the next night they went out to dinner together. That was quite a while ago and now they are married. I have heard that sometimes step-parents and step-children do not get along but we sure do because he likes me and I like him, most of the time.

Sometimes at dinner we talk about how we became a family. I love it when we do that. What if I had gone to some other dentist? Or what if I never had the toothache at all? And what if our favorite friends back home had not been named Brown?

If you could see my mother and new father holding hands in church I know you would feel like the three of us do. All of us believe the only way it could happen was for God to think it up. My grandparents think so, too. It could never have been an accident.

My mother says an angel guided her hand that day she was looking up dentists in the phone book.

I hope an angel does something as wonderful as that for you sometime.

I forgot to tell you another thing my stepfather said that shows how nice he is. He said if I ever get a toothache again, he would fix it and not even charge us anything.

Hannah

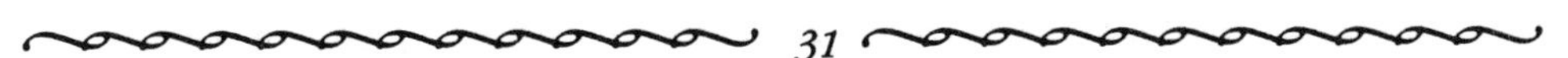

Who Were Those Two Men in White?

Did you know a tractor can sometimes tip over with the driver still on it? It happened to my father. I saw it. He was going up a small grade which means something like a little hill. All at once the tractor reared up and over. My father could not get off. He hung on and ended up under the tractor. What could he do?

It is lucky my father is a strong man and his legs are his strongest part. When it happened, I ran out to the field. There he was holding the tractor up with his legs. It was not a big tractor, but big enough. I didn't know what to do. Then all at once here came two men running across the field.

If you saw where we live, you would wonder where these two came from. The only road by our house is gravel and hardly anybody drives on it. We don't have close neighbors and we're a long way from town. But here they came. When they got to us it didn't take them hardly any time at all to lift up the tractor for my father to crawl out. Of course my father thanked them and invited them to dinner at our house. But they said they couldn't come because they had to be going. Dad asked their names but they just waved and went off down the road. We didn't see a car, a truck, or anything to ride in.

We have some neighbors who are our best friends. They are very religious, but we don't go to church. That is why I was surprised when my father wanted to go ask our neighbors what they knew about angels. My mother and I went along. When my father told them what happened, they said, "Of course the two men were angels." And they gave us their reasons. They said angels show up all of a sudden and out of nowhere. They said angels are to help people and anyone with a tractor on top of them needs help, don't they? They also said angels usually dress in white.

Well, we've talked about this a lot and my father's decided we should start going to our neighbors' church so we can learn more about angels. My mother and I think this is a good idea.

Raymond

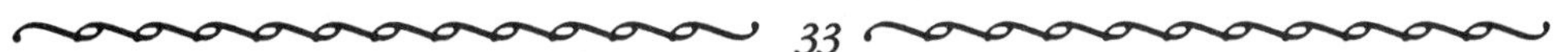

"Except Ye Become as Little Children..."

Jarrett: *"I like this story."*

Grandpa: *"I like it, too. But I have some questions for you. How is it that angels show up so often at exactly the right time?"*

Jarrett: *"I wonder if it could be like this? Say there are angels everywhere and they are all assigned certain territories. So maybe every territory has a chief angel up in heaven to see everything going on in that area. Then when there is an accident this chief angel sends messages to the earth angels. He signals them where the accident is and that's how they get there so fast. Of course I don't know for sure if this is how they work, but it could be, couldn't it?"*

Grandpa: *"Sure could. But here's another problem. Raymond says his family isn't religious. Why would angels come to help him?"*

Jarrett: *"That's no problem, Grandpa. You know God loves everybody whether they love him back or not."*

On the Wings of a Dove

Part Two

When the Angels Must Cry with Us

Were you ever left to cry alone? No one to share your sadness with? No one to talk with you? No one? Then, suddenly, there was a presence to comfort you.

Did the Yellow Light Spell "Love"?

How many times was I scolded, screamed at, whipped and put to bed without my supper? How many nights did my parents lock me in my room, pull down the blinds and leave me in darkness? Too, too many.

How old was I? Since I hadn't started school, I couldn't have been more than five. One memorable night, something very special happened.

I had been whipped harder than usual that particular night and sent to bed. On most mornings I awoke from a fitful sleep of terrible dreams. But on this morning I could remember clearly only one peaceful dream of comfort. In that dream I saw a yellow light, a bright light, brilliant. A mellow light, comforting to soothe my bruised boy heart.

So healing, so enfolding it was, and I remember pleading, "Please, don't go away, ever."

From that time on when I had been whipped and put to bed in my darkened room, the light returned as I slept. Then one night I saw dim movement in the light and I remember saying to myself, "This must be an angel come to help me."

Now as I listened, I heard a voice, dim at first but a real voice. Only the voice didn't seem to come from up there, out there, off there. Instead as I tuned to its sound, I knew the source was inside me, and this is what I heard:

"You must not hate your parents. The awful feeling they have for you is not your fault. Something is wrong inside them and if you hate them that same thing will be wrong in you. You must find someone who needs love like *you* need love. If you will find that someone and love them you will feel loved too."

Could a five-year-old hear something like that? And how could he understand even if he heard it? Would he possibly have the wisdom to comprehend all this?

Now, meet Malcolm. Malcolm was crippled. Why are children so cruel? Why would everyone in our class tease him because he couldn't walk straight? Why would they mimic him, make fun of his little walker, laugh at his twisted body and his limp? And why couldn't they get the lonely message from his heart when he stood on the playground watching us at our games? Poor Malcolm. So sad. So rejected. So alone.

Watching Malcolm I remembered the yellow light and heard the voice again, clear, from inside me. "Be Malcolm's friend. You be nice to him and maybe the others will too. Make him a special friend. See what happens."

So that's what I did, and you will know what followed. Malcolm and I became best friends. The more I loved him, the more he loved me and that was wonderful, exactly like the inner voice said. And the more we loved each other, the more our whole class loved.

I am an old man now. The light is still shining in my memory, but that's not all. After all these years of musing it has become a part of me, an actuality in my soul. More and more clearly I hear angels whispering:

Blessings come back to the blesser,
Gifts return to the giver
And always, no exception,
Love circles back to the lover.
This is the law of the Lord.

"Tervetuola"

My sister, Annie, was very sick. For a long time she was sick with bone cancer and oh, how she hurt. Operation after operation she hurt, and I hurt with her. But I think it was even harder for our mom and dad. Sometimes, late at night when we had all gone to bed, I could hear them talking. Crying, too. About Annie. About the bills. How could they know what to do about either of these things?

Then came the time when Annie started to improve. We all decided we would invite an exchange student from Finland to come live with us. Jaana was beautiful with blond hair and blue eyes. I'm not very pretty, but she taught me how to use makeup when my parents weren't looking. It made me feel special.

That spring Jaana's parents planned to visit us all the way from Finland. We were really excited, and so were they. My dad made a welcome sign we put across the front of our house. *Tervetuola* it said, which is "welcome" in Finnish.

Then Annie became sick again and had to have another operation. This one was even more serious. It cost a lot of money. About a week before Jaana's parents arrived, I heard mom and dad talking about how we would ever feed our guests. We were out of money and didn't have much "guest food" in the cupboard.

The next day was Sunday. At breakfast dad said we must ask God to help us take care of our guests. So we held hands and prayed. Dad had always said we shouldn't say anything at church about our money problems. This was a firm rule. He didn't want people feeling sorry for us. He reminded us not to say anything this time, too. And we didn't.

When we came home from church later that day, we saw our front porch door propped open. When we got out of the car to take a closer look, you'll never guess! There on the porch were eight big boxes. All full, full of groceries. All kinds of groceries. Ham, cheese, beef, bread, vegetables. Even a big chocolate cake! My mother cried, and my dad cleared his throat like he does when he has a lump. You can imagine we thanked God with all our hearts that day for being so good to us.

We never did figure out for sure who sent the food. None of our friends knew. But I think I know. God sent a Finnish angel to us. He knew our house by the "welcome" sign.

Elaine

"Except Ye Become as Little Children . . ."

Grandpa: *"Elaine talks about Finnish angels. Do you think there are different kinds of angels for different kinds of people?"*

Jarrett: *"Of course there are. I read a book about Alabama angels and they talked just like people from Alabama."*

Grandpa: *"Elaine says none of her friends knew about the trouble her family was having and her father was too proud to tell anybody at church. Could it be the angels knew and brought all the food?"*

Jarrett: *"It doesn't sound like angels to me. I think what happened is an angel told someone at church and they told someone else and soon everybody at church brought food. I don't see angels carrying food if they can get a person to do it. It's good for people to do things for other people. And angels like to help people be their best."*

Prayer:

Lord, help me to live every day, every year
In the beautiful spirit of "tervetuola." *Amen*

On the Wings of a Dove

Diane grew up in a home with little religious training. She didn't go to church or Sunday School. No blessings at mealtime, no evening prayers, no open Bible. No concept of religious symbolism, no training in things spiritual.

When she was ten years old her family moved from town to a beautiful house on the country hill overlooking their village. Diane's upper level room was one story up from her parents'. For the first time, she was not on the same floor with them.

Now in her own words:

"It had been cozy living in town. I could look out my bedroom window and see the friendly lights of our neighbors all up and down the street. And it was comforting to know my folks were just down the hall. Then we moved and this was something else. By day my new country room was a dream, but in the dark it became a nightmare.

"As cars rounded the cemetery bend on the next hill, headlights would circle my room making spooky designs.... The chair became a monster. One shoe looked like a huge insect. Everywhere the lights made dragons, murderers, wild animals.

"Night after night the same ritual. Fearfully, I would get down on all fours, then quickly lift the dust ruffle to catch a glance of whatever might be lurking under the bed. Next I would sneak up on my closet and fling it open to scare away the nasties inside. Another door led to an attic off my room, but I never touched that door. It was too scary! I would push my chair against it, turn off my light, and jump in bed. Then I would shiver and peer from under the covers into the darkness. I would try to sleep with the blankets scrunched around my ears.

"Then one night a new light came. This one didn't circle the room. It stayed in place. It fascinated me because it had a distinct shape. I called it my white dove. Watching it, my fears subsided and I drifted off into peaceful dreams because somehow I felt the dove would guard me against any danger.

"From that scary room I moved to college dorms and then into homes of my own. Never again have I felt fear at night. Why? Because I carry in my memory the vision of a white dove transforming the darkness. This was my very own personal dove of peace.

"Now as a Christian, I know God was doing more than comforting my fears. He was preparing me to welcome his Dove, the Prince of Peace, into my heart."

Diane

"Except Ye Become as Little Children . . ."

Grandpa: *"Diane never said she saw an angel, did she? What she saw was a dove. Could this have been an angel?"*

Jarrett: *"Sure, angels can come any way they want to. They come as birds, animals, people, anything. It doesn't matter. They come to let someone know God cares about them. That's pretty neat, isn't it?"*

Prayer:

Lord, make me ever alert to the brush of an angel's wing anytime, anywhere, in any living creature. *Amen*

"You Don't Need to Worry Anymore"

His name was Ronnie. He had come with his parents to an event called "An Evening with the Angels." It's a fun time for reviewing my book, *Brush of an Angel's Wing*. I had told some of my favorite stories and we listened as others shared. Soon we arrived at the question-and-answer time. Fascinating questions of every ilk, deep and pensive. People these days are avidly interested in angels. How do they work? What are they, really? Will I ever actually *see* one?

When it was closing time, Ronnie stood to ask, "Can I talk?" Of course he could, and we waited with high anticipation. Out of the mouths of babes cometh all kinds of interesting information. No exception this time.

"My name is Ronnie and I am eight. I *know* there are angels and I will tell you how I know. My grandma was my favorite person and she died two years ago. But sometimes she comes back to my room in the night and I know it's her because she is wearing her red robe and every time she comes there is an angel with her. It is always the same angel dressed in white. I think she is a lady angel and she's younger than my grandmother. She has wings and is always smiling.

"I have listened to all of you talk and I feel sorry because it seems like some of you can hardly believe in angels and whether they are real or not. That's why I want to tell you about my grandma and her angel friend. Now *you don't have to worry anymore!* I thought you would like to know that."

Ronnie

Did Ronnie really "see" his grandmother?

Let's have a look at that.

Brush of an Angel's Wing ends with a simple invitation for readers to share their angel stories with me. Response? A trainload, a ton, a zillion witnesses writing from their hearts. And if you could read my mail, you'd know Ronnie's claim of seeing a loved one after death is multiplied ad infinitim.

But did all these witnesses actually "see" with their eyes? Were they hallucinating? Were these viewings real?

This is my belief: after our loved ones die, we don't actually "see" them anymore with our eyes. Yet our memories are powerful. So powerful they are strong enough to produce an "inner vision." By that inner vision we are still connected to the soul of our loved ones.

In this sense I had some very real experiences of seeing my Martha. For at least a year after her death, my inner vision brought her to me. Sometimes I would be awakened from my sleep and there she was. Often she would be wearing her big yellow sweater; the same one I remember from the first time I saw her in ninth grade. But I saw her in other places too: skating, taking pecan rolls out of the oven, smiling beside me in the car, praying, even stepping from the shower.

Is all this too far out? Not for those of us who loved with an everlasting love, it isn't. Actually, forty-eight years of a "heaven on earth" marriage would make a forever and forever imprint on the mind, the heart, the soul, wouldn't it?

Say it again. *In this sense* I believe all my reporters "saw." Ronnie did. I did.

You do understand that I am not an authority on all this. Who am I to say how another person might "see" or not see their loved one after death? I only know for sure that *I did*. And if I did, what actually was going on inside me? For answers, I've talked with psychiatrists, psychologists, physicians, writers, and fellow clergy. Children, young adults, middle aged, senior citizens, and the very old: I sought counsel from them too. In groups and with individuals I've asked questions. In depth I followed up certain of the witnesses for more input. And this is my conclusion:

I believe the good Lord, who first thought up you and me and all his children, blessed us this way too—he equipped us with inner eyes for holy recall to comfort, guide, warn, bless, and be thankful.

Prayer of a Grateful Heart:

O divine Creator, thank you for the inner vision
whereby we see the unseen and comprehend
the unknowable. *Amen.*

"Why Would You Do That, Dale?"

Part Three

The Awesome Wisdom of Cherub Chatter

Out of the mouths of babes cometh many good things. Cometh correction. Cometh all kinds of funnies. Out of the mouths of little boys like Jarrett cometh the profound. Thank you, Lord, for children's perspectives uncomplicating our adult confusion.

When the little ones talk about angels, I'd better listen. Why? I'd better listen because those we call youngsters might be wise beyond their years. They might even know more about proper adult behavior than I know!

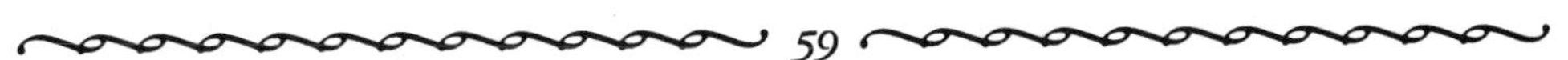

Can Angels Chew Snuff?

My father calls my mother an angel, but I don't think she is because she chews snuff. Snuff is something like chewing tobacco. Do you know how people who chew tobacco spit all the time? Well, my mother sure does spit a lot. I have thought about this and how my Sunday School teacher says angels come out mostly at night. That's when they usually came in the Bible. Well, if they fly around spitting that would be pretty messy, wouldn't it? I don't think real angels would do that. That's why I don't think my mother could be an angel.

Calvin

Right on, Calvin! Every one of us, child and adult, needs your lesson about keeping ourselves in shape for the angels. A major responsibility for all of us, isn't it?

60

"Why Would You Do That, Dale?"

Archer Heights Presbyterian Church in Chicago was my first student pastorate at Seminary. A small congregation, it was made up of Polish Protestants, some of them recent immigrants. They loved to celebrate. So special holy seasons in this little church were exciting. I will forever remember one particular event.

On this night we were deep in our Christmas pageant. Our director was one of Chicago's leading ballerinas. A member of our church, she gave her talent to produce a Christmas pageant like we had never seen before.

The church was packed. We were down to the final scene. All of us were in awe of the smooth production, plus spiritual atunement of the highest order.

Here the children came, each to his or her own marked spot on stage. Chalked letters on the floor told the children where to stand. "A" for Angels, "S" for Shepherds, "W" for Wise Men, down to "X" for all the little extra boys and girls who needed their places too.

Suddenly, just as the music started, one little boy with a mighty blow floored the angel standing in front of him. Down she went, flat, screaming. To the horror of everyone, with a resounding crash, down went the spiritual high.

The angel girl cried while the audience sat stunned. The entire cast watched in panic as up from the audience rushed the little boy's mother. Seizing her son in a fierce grip, she began shaking him, screaming over and over in high pitch: "Why would you do that, Dale? Why ever would you do that? You ruined the whole show." Enter now the director to join the screaming, "You've devastated our pageant, Dale. Why? Why ever would you?"

At last, with mother and director out of breath, out of energy, and out of questions, came the clear voice of little Dale answering,

"That blankety-blank angel was standing on my X."

Obviously, decency forbids my telling you what Dale's "blankety-blank" was in actuality. Suffice it to say it was akin to what my Uncle Edgar would have labelled "a Jim Dandy toe-curler."

The result? Chaos for the moment, but for long-range benefits? Planned by an expert choreographer, it couldn't have been better publicity for any community of believers. Never better for story telling time round the fireplace or kitchen table. Super tale to be told at the factory and grocery store. But that's not all. Through sixty-five years of pastoral recall, never better for laughs.

Thank you, Dale, thank you.

"Except Ye Become as Little Children . . ."

What is the lesson for today, children?
The lesson for today is:
As you go through life make sure you're not
standing on somebody's X.

What is the lesson, parents?
Best we should watch our language at home.
(In all fairness to Dale, I knew his mother!!!)

"What Did She Put on My Sister's Face?"

We were camping at a state park in Tennessee. We are a close family and we do this every summer. My father is an insurance salesman and my mother a schoolteacher. There are five of us with my two sisters and me.

My father was grilling hamburgers when all of a sudden my little sister came running down the road, screaming. Blood was all over her face because she was cut just awful. When she ran up to us we could tell she'd fallen into some glass. Some of the glass was still sticking from her face and her hands. You could tell it hurt a lot.

My father ran to the office to ask for help. But they told him the nearest hospital was twelve miles away. She was bleeding so much, we had to do something right away. By now lots of campers were coming to see what was wrong, but nobody knew what to do. Then sort of like from nowhere a tall lady came right up to us and offered to help, "I have some salve I can put on her face to make her stop bleeding. It will also keep her from hurting anymore."

She was tall and kind of thin, but not too thin. She was a beautiful lady with very dark hair and dark skin too. She also had a beautiful smile and there was something about her eyes, something that made us believe she knew what she was doing and she really could help my sister.

Well, what would you do? My folks decided they would let the lady go ahead. Someone stretched a blanket on the picnic table and put my sister on it. Then the lady took what looked like thick dark chocolate and rubbed it all over my sister's face and hands. The dark lady hardly said anything at all but all the time she was putting the stuff on my sister's face she kept singing soft and low. My sister quit crying right away and after a little while she went to sleep.

Of course all of us were looking at my sister because we were amazed at how quickly her bleeding stopped. Nobody saw the lady slip away. She was gone before we could thank her or find out what the salve was.

My sister slept all night and in the morning she was fine. There was no glass sticking in her skin and we could hardly tell where she had been cut. And she never got any scars. Not one.

All this was four years ago and we don't know what really happened any more now than we did then. Of course we talk about it a lot and one of the things we always ask is something you probably would ask too: *"Was the lady with the salve an angel?"*

My father and mother and all of us are real religious people. Like I said, my father is an insurance salesman but in our church he is also what is called a Lay Preacher. I have heard him talk about the lady and my sister many times. He always asks, "Do you think that lady was an angel? Well, there must have been an angel somewhere. If your child was healed overnight, I think you might pray this same prayer we pray real often in our family devotions: 'Thank you, God, for your angels.'"

Jackie

"Except Ye Become as Little Children . . ."

Grandpa: *"Do you think the lady was an angel, Jarrett? Where did she come from?"*

Jarrett: *"I don't think she was an angel."*

Oh, woe, there goes my angel story, I thought. Just as I was about to conclude we'd lost this one. Then after one of his long pauses Jarrett gave me another lesson in the wonder of child theology.

Jarrett: *"I think she was a lady in the camp who heard the little girl crying. And she was the kind of woman who would have to find out why."*

Grandpa: *"Sounds good. How do you explain the brown salve?"*

Jarrett: *"I think an angel brought it to her and told her to go put it on the little girl."*

Grandpa: *"OK. But why would the angel choose this particular lady?"*

Jarrett: *"Why not? Angels know who they should use. They use people who love everybody. They could even tell the lady what songs to sing, couldn't they? And that brown salve? Do you remember when Jesus took some mud and put it on a man's eyes and the man could see? Why couldn't it be the angel brought some of that same stuff and gave it to the lady?"*

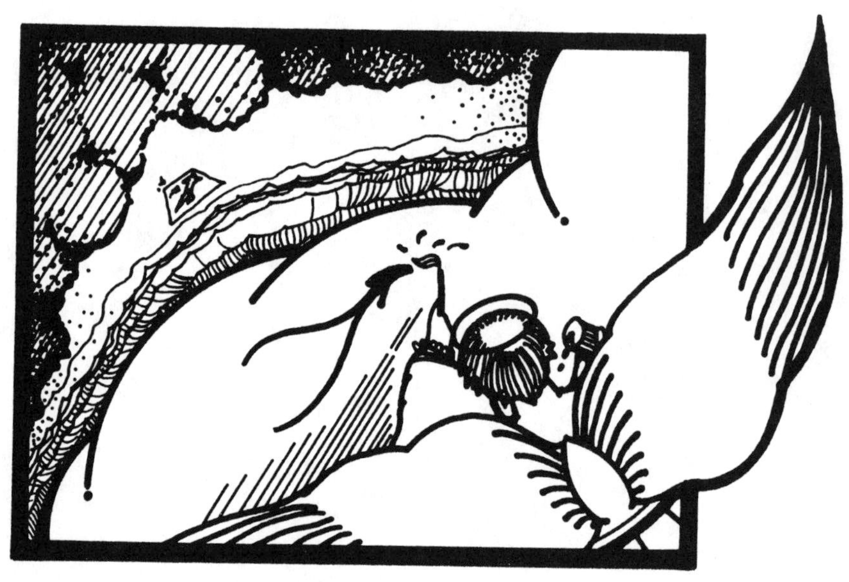

Angels Who Draw Pictures in the Clouds

Part Four

Three Stories from a Northern Lake

If some day you are done in, discouraged, ready to call it quits—if your hope is down and you almost don't care anymore—go sit by a lake and be very still.

Listen to the sounds: birds calling to birds, frogs croaking to frogs, fish jumping. Are they showing their skills, giving signals? Or are they simply celebrating the goodness of being alive, thanking God for their lake?

And the clouds. Have you ever spent an entire afternoon lying at lakeside watching the sky pictures change? Libby was only fifteen but she must have been the world's number one watcher of clouds… she was also number one at what they could tell us. Libby believed there were special angels in the heavenly film room constantly changing the sky for our entertainment. Do you believe that?

"Alone on the Rock" was a young Indian boy who caught fish without a pole, without bait, without net. He believed what his grandfather taught him: there are angels who, if we let them be our friends, will teach us things we could never know without them.

The superintendent of this state park where we cabined had a daughter. Her name was Rachel. She was in first grade. She went to school by bus and every night her special friend came out of the woods to walk with her. All the way from the bus stop, down the long lane to her home, he would walk with her. She would play church with him. She would sit on a stump and sing. She would tell him Bible stories from their family devotions. He would sit before her in the road, cocking his head this way, that way. Did he understand that God is so wonderful? She thought he did.

Here are three stories from a northern lake.

The Big, Big Kitty

Those were great summers when our children were small and we vacationed at Camp Burnside in Duluth, Minnesota. Majestic setting: tall trees, very tall. Majestic view: clear cold water, blue lake. Good swimming, good fishing, good people at Burnside. And one of those good people told us this story.

Each year the camp superintendent invited us to his home for dinner. One night the superintendent asked us to listen while his little girl told her story, which he called "The Big, Big Kitty."

Each spring after the snow melted, wildlife began their moving about, sometimes in unexpected places, unexpected ways. This is his daughter's story:

"Every afternoon the big kitty would meet me at the school bus stop. Then we would walk up the long lane together through the woods to our house. Of course

I told my parents and big brother about it and my father asked me to describe the big kitty.

"So I said, 'He is brown and gray and the biggest cat I ever saw. He has pointed ears and eyes that look kind of pointed too, so he is different from any cat I ever saw. Besides that, he doesn't have a tail. He is very nice because he walks real close to me. Only he won't let me touch him. If I try, he just moves away. I talk to him and I think he likes that, only he never makes a sound.'

"Sometimes I sit on a stump and play church with him. I tell him Bible stories and sing songs. Do you know what he does? He just listens and turns his head one way and then the other. So I know he likes it. I've tried to get him to come all the way to our porch for some food, but he always goes away as soon as we get near the house. Then I see him the next afternoon just up the lane from where the bus lets me off and he walks me home again. I like that and I think he does too."

Rachel

What would you do now if you were her father? Probably you'd do what he did. "For four afternoons," he said, "I stood behind a tree waiting and watching. But those four days the big kitty never came. Then the fifth day I climbed a tree to watch. Sure enough, there he came to meet my little girl. It was just like she said. He walked beside her, looked up at her when she talked to him, but moved away when she reached for him. No doubt about it! The big, big kitty was a big, big bobcat!"

We held our breath when we asked the superintendent what he did next. "I stun-gunned him."

What does that mean? Our family once lived on an island where they shot the overabundance of deer with tranquilizer guns. Stunned, the deer were trucked away to other parks. That's what he had done with the big, big kitty.

But we very much like what Rachel's mother said.

"I think," she smiled, "there must have been a special angel walking with them every afternoon, don't you?"

"Except Ye Become as Little Children . . ."

Grandpa: *"Why do you think a wild bobcat would want to be with Rachel?"*

Jarrett: *"I think an angel sent him."*

Grandpa: *"But I don't understand why an angel would do that."*

Jarrett: *"Grandpa, you don't have to understand. Maybe that little girl needed help. Don't you know children sometimes need help, too?"*

Grandpa: *"What kind of help do you think a girl might need from a bobcat?"*

Jarrett: *"Well, maybe she was having a hard time at school. She thought her teacher didn't like her or some other kid in the class teased her or she didn't understand something. So the angel sent the bobcat to let her know someone cared. And didn't her father say this was spring when all the wildlife came out? Maybe there was a bear in the woods or a wolf. The bobcat could have come to scare them away. See?"*

Grandpa: *"Yes, I see."*

For pondering

Wouldn't it be wonderful if we would never outgrow the mind of that little child in us? Jesus said, "Anyone who will not receive the kingdom of God like a little child will never enter it."

Mark 10:15

Angels Who Draw Pictures in the Clouds

Libby was a chubby sophomore, aged fifteen. Her beautiful smile was so pleasant that, on her, even "chubby" looked good. She was an obvious lover of everything she surveyed and she missed very little of what she surveyed. She especially loved the clouds and their pictures.

In the first three grades at St. Mary by the Lake she had been trained to see the clouds. Her teacher, Sister Grace, was an expert in the art of "reading the sky." One of "Sister's" goals was to have her students become cloud experts too. Libby must have been one of her best pupils ever.

This is how we met Libby. At our vacation camp, high school girls were hired to keep the cabins tidy. Girls with personality-plus could also serve as guides. The big lake was ultra cold, which our children loved, but much too shivery for adults. We preferred quiet lakes and warmer swimming waters. No problem for Libby. "The Land of Ten Thousand Lakes" had plenty from which to choose.

So here we were sitting in Libby's rowboat, enjoying this sunny day, utterly relaxed. "Now," she began, "I will show you what the Cloud Angels have drawn for us today."

"See? Up there is a mother fox and her two little foxes."

"Right, Libby. So plain it can be nothing but a fox and her two little foxes."

"Over here behind us, see it coming. You watch. A city with tall skyscrapers, streets, and even some cars moving. A park and houses around it. Watch now. They will form for you.

"See those three big clouds? Don't they look like geese flying way off there? And there's a deer with his antlers raised. Look at the man lying down with his eyes closed. And here comes an elephant. Angels don't draw like we do. They draw whatever comes to their minds and that's why it's so much fun. Sister Grace said they do it this way so every day there will be something new in the clouds for us to discover."

Cats and dogs, sheep and rabbits, children running and a man fishing. A child swinging, the lady sweeping, two boys fighting, the cannon going off. On and on and on. And up to that day in our lives wasn't this one of our greatest days ever?

Late that afternoon, when we said good-bye at the dock, Libby hugged us as we thanked her. We told her this was one day for sure we'd never forget. Then she stepped back, took our hands, and said one more unforgettable jewel:

"Do you know why there are pictures in the clouds? Has anyone ever told you why? The reason is that God has artist angels drawing in the clouds. This is what Sister Grace taught us. She said that *God loves us so much he wants us to have fun even when we're studying the clouds.*"

Alone on a Rock

He was a handsome young Indian boy. Dark skin, dark hair, dark eyes. He stood straight as his ancestor's arrows flew. We would never forget his magnificent smile that matched the sun coming up behind him. And every morning on his back he carried the biggest string of fish we ever saw. That is no casual statement, friend. Martha and I grew up on the Cedar River which flowed through our town. We had seen fish, fish, fish but never a single fisher's string like this.

They were exactly alike, every fish like the other fish, no exception. "All skillet size," he smiled as he took them down for our examination. "You eat fish?" he asked. "I deliver every morning to the cabins. Where are you staying? If you like I will come to you."

Of course we liked. Anyone who grew up on the Cedar River would like fish. So we made a deal. His name was Trevor, and by the way he shook hands we knew every morning he would be there. Almost the exact time every morning there he was with our fish, every one skillet size.

Sometimes he obviously planned his route so he would deliver last to our place. This seemed to be the Indian way of saying, "We are friends. I want to know you. I want you to know me." It was one great friendship.

The day we told him I was a minister, something inside Trevor beamed a bright light. Obviously a special light from far down the roads of his history. With great reverence he announced that his grandfather had been a minister, a Christian minister. So had his great-grandfather. Trevor was a firm believer, but he would not follow in their footsteps. He would be a doctor.

Then he smiled his most beautiful smile as he said, "My grandfather gave me my other name. *Alone on a Rock.*"

"But why? Why would you be named 'Alone on a Rock'?"

"If you like I will show you." He said it proudly, as if he were handing us a key to a sacred room in his Native American heritage.

So we accepted his invitation. We would meet him the next day and he would show us how he fished. We wondered how many people had ever been invited to see him fish.

As we walked along the path the next morning, he explained how it would be. We should sit with him on his rock, but we must be very still. No talking. No whispering. No movement. Absolute silence. Somehow as he spoke we felt we were about to enter a sacred cathedral of oneness with the creation. Very sacred.

He helped us up on his chosen rock and motioned for us to be seated. Quietly, right there behind him, we took our places. But how would he fish? No pole. No net. No throw line. Nothing in his hand; absolutely nothing. Yet too late to ask now. Absolute silence, remember? He was about to fish.

First, though, he must pray. And this was prayer at its purest. There he sat, legs crossed, arms raised to heaven, eyes up too. And before we knew it, we were doing the same. Turning to smile at us, he laid himself prone on the rock and lowered his long right arm into the water. Far down.

Next he motioned us forward. Look. In the clear, clear water were more fish than we had ever seen in one place. Giant fish, small fish, and countless "skillet size." There was very little movement, except for one thing. Up and down, back and forth, very slowly "Alone on a Rock" was moving his middle finger. Later he told us he was hypnotizing the fish, as if to some inner metronome.

Softly a single fish would come closer, and the hand would move toward it. Tenderly the finger would stroke the fish, and then slip gently into the gill. Then he would flip that fish out of the water, catch it, string it. One more fish for his line, and in all the time we watched he never missed.

Over and over, same process, next fish. But why didn't those fish dart away with the splash? They did. But almost at once they returned again to be mesmerized by the finger. Over and over, until he had his catch for the day.

"Whoever taught you this? How long did it take to learn? How old were you when you started? Don't they ever bite your hand?"

"No, they don't bite me. I must make them believe I am one of them. I was seven when my grandfather taught me. He was an old man and had time for me. It took much time to learn."

Every summer Trevor would welcome us and invite us again to watch him fish. Then one year came the compliment supreme: WE WERE INVITED TO HIS HOME. He was proud as he gave us the note from his mother. Would we honor them with our presence?

It was a wonderful evening and an unforgettable dinner. Fish baked in corn, plus other interesting native dishes. We swapped legends and stories, sang hymns, and ate some more. Truly unforgettable all the way.

Later that evening, Trevor asked if we would like to see his room. Of course we would. Out back, a little place by itself. Inside, quiet earth colors, and we especially liked the rich red of his sleeping mat.

But over there on the wall, a centerpiece. What was it? Not ceramic. Not metal. Some special kind of wood? Yes.

"My grandfather and I found it in the marsh and brought it here together. It's petrified wood. If you'll sit here with me long enough, you will see."

Ah! An angel. "See the head, the eyes, the shadow of a smile? There are the arms, the hands, the body. And look—wings!" But when we looked away, the angel seemed to disappear. Once more, only a plain wooden figure. Old wood from the swamp. "Close your eyes now. Look once more. The angel will return and smile for you again." And he did!

Next we asked, "Do you actually communicate with your angel, Trevor? Do you talk with each other?"

"Oh, yes. We start every morning that way. But now I must answer you with care. I almost always let my angel speak first, and I listen. I also ask questions and if I listen closely, from far down inside, I will know what is right.

"All this my grandfather taught me. Our Heavenly Father is a loving God who sends his angels to help us. I could not fish if I did not believe there are *special angels for the fishermen."**

**Author's Note:* Does this surprise you? It shouldn't. How many times does the Bible verify this kind of meditation? I will not spoil such an exciting search for you. But I will give you a clue: You will find many answers in both Old Testament and New.

After Martha and I went fishing with Trevor we added this to our Bible study time: "Did Jesus know how to catch fish with his hands?" For an answer we would turn to the "Fisherman's Chapter," John 21.

It was early morning and Jesus came to the beach. The disciples had been fishing all night and caught nothing. Not far out now, they heard a familiar call, "Any fish, boys?" To a negative response Jesus said, "Throw your net on the right side of the boat… you'll get plenty" (see verses 5-6). They did, and he was right!

Lesson one:

My Lord knows more about everything than I know.

When the disciples arrived back on the shore, Jesus said, "Bring some of the fish you have now caught." Why would he do this? Verse 9 tells us he already had fish frying. So…

Lesson two:

For every relationship, my fish plus your fish make a better breakfast for us all than eating my fish alone.

Some things are so pensive they need time for deep meditation, and this for me will forever be one such question: Did Jesus know how to catch fish with his hands?

That Unseen Hand on My Shoulder

Part Five

Angels to the Rescue

Let others call it "luck." Let cynics label it "chance." But could it be that our children are closer to the truth when they talk of "Power Rangers," "Super Heroes," or "Ninja" good guys? Does it matter what we call those fantastic creatures that conquer evil to make life good again? By any name, couldn't they be angels of the Lord?

How Did That Angel Get over the Fence?

Dear Dr. Charlie Shedd,

I enjoyed reading your book *Brush of an Angel's Wing*. As I finished I noticed the invitation in the back and wanted to respond.

My name is Amy. Gina is my friend. Two years ago Gina and I were coming home from high school. It was pouring down rain to the point that we couldn't see in front of us. Avoiding all low water crossings, we were trying to find the safest way home. But after we turned left at the stop sign, we looked at each other and knew we were in trouble.

We were in the water and our car wouldn't move. We were shocked to see the water was already covering the hood. Next it came up to the door handle. Every kind of emotion overwhelmed us. Water began seeping in and soon it was covering the floormats. But we couldn't get out because the water pressure was too great to open our doors.

We knew the situation was beyond us so we bowed our heads in prayer. We asked God to please send us help. Then as we finished praying, we looked up to see a young man riding his bicycle in the middle of the street. He was coming straight at us, trapped in the low spot. We were almost afraid to open the window for fear water would come rushing in. But finally we dared it and he said, "My name is Dave and I came to help you." Then he gave us his hand and we climbed out the window. He even held up our purses as we trudged through the water together.

When we came to the side of the street, Dave looked at the car and rising water. He asked if we wanted the window rolled up. We told him not to worry about it, and we headed toward some apartments. These were the kind with a high fence and gate locked tight.

While we were talking about how to get through the locked gate, Dave was suddenly on the other side turning the lock. Then he opened it for us and we walked through. But when we turned to thank him, he was gone. Vanished completely.

So we knocked on a door and these folks, recognizing an emergency, let us in to phone our parents. Then we went back near the car to get our bookbags. But the water was still too high to open the door, and what a surprise to find the window rolled up all the way.

How could Dave have rolled up that window without opening the door? And what could have become of him? As long as we live, Gina and I will believe Dave was a real angel, an angel on a bicycle, sent to rescue us.

Amy

"Except Ye Become as Little Children . . ."

Grandpa: *"How come an angel came on a bicycle?"*

Jarrett: *"Well, angels need some fun, too. He probably borrowed it from someone."*

Grandpa: *"How'd he get over that fence?"*

Jarrett: *"Oh, angels move real fast. He took off his jacket, pulled out his wings, flew over, and put on his jacket again so fast they didn't see it! I think when angels are helping people they can do anything they want, so speedy nobody would see them. There are people like that in the movies, you know. And angels have got to be better than people in the movies."*

Would an Angel Drive a Cadillac?

My father drives a big truck and sometimes he goes on long trips. Last year he had a serious back operation. This is not a good thing because somebody who drives such a big truck has to lift heavy stuff all the time.

It is lucky my father drives for a company with a very nice boss. The boss likes my father a lot because he has driven safely a long time. When he could drive after his operation, the boss hired someone else to lift things into the truck. Then when my father got where he was going, the boss had somebody there to lift everything off. I think that was nice, don't you?

Now I will tell you what happened that wasn't so nice, but it turned out real good. I can say this because I was with my father when it happened. I am twelve years old and I know a lot about trucks. So even though his company does not usually allow riders, sometimes I go along to help my father.

Here is the bad part. We were way out west where there are not many towns. Suddenly we heard this loud bang. A tire blowout. Some tires, when they blow out, you can still go on because there is another tire right beside it. But this time when we got out to look, we could see the blown out tire was a single. That meant we couldn't go on until we put on a new tire.

Right away you can see the problem. Taking the blown tire off and putting the spare on would be a hard job for my father with his bad back. It'd even be hard for someone with a good back. First, you have to get out the jack and it is heavy. Then you jack up the side where the tire is flat. You take off the heavy old tire. Finally, you get down the good spare tire, lift it on the wheel, and tighten it up. It is heavy. Everything on a truck is real heavy.

Well, all of a sudden something wonderful happened. We could hardly believe it! A car stopped and a nice-looking man got out. He was all dressed up like he had been to a party or to church or something like that. He asked what the matter was and my father showed him. The man just laughed and said, "No problem. I can fix that quick." And he did.

My father and I decided the man must have changed lots of tires. He got the blown out tire off easily. Then he lifted the spare right on and fit it to the lugs quickly. He also did another thing which made us know he had changed tires before. He put all the tools away in the tool box just where they were supposed to be.

All this time the man didn't say anything. He hummed and whistled. But when we asked questions like where was he from, he just smiled and kept on working. He didn't ask us our names or where we were heading. We wondered later if he already knew that. When my father offered to pay him, which you should always do, he just laughed and shook his head. Did I tell you he also smiled most of the time and laughed a lot? He must have been a very happy man.

I guess I should tell you some other things we noticed about him. One was his clothes. They never got dirty. He was wearing a light tan shirt and pants, almost white. They never got one bit dirty. That is not at all how it is normally. If you change a truck tire, you get real dirty. The other thing we noticed was that he was driving a brand new Cadillac. It was white too.

Whoever do you suppose he was? I wish I could tell you but I can't. My father and I have talked a lot about this man and we feel almost sure he was an angel. What else could such a nice man be?

But then we always come back to this question:

Do you think an angel would be driving a new white Cadillac?

Thad

"Except Ye Become as Little Children . . ."

Grandpa: *"Tell me, Jarrett. Would an angel be driving a white Cadillac?"*

Jarrett: *"Of course. What other color would he drive?"*

Grandpa: *"But why would he be on that road at the time when this man needed help?"*

Jarrett: *"Because that's when he needed help."*

Grandpa: *"But a Cadillac? Jarrett, I've never even owned a Cadillac."*

Jarrett: *"But Grandpa, angels don't think like people, and you are a people! Well, maybe there was this movie star who made piles of money and that particular angel helped him get an Oscar. Whoever the movie star was told the angel, 'Thank you, thank you. If you ever need my help, let me know.' So the angel knew this movie star had bought a white Cadillac, and the angel always wanted to drive a white Cadillac. They probably don't have white Cadillacs in heaven. So he thought he'd have some fun and use the white Cadillac to go help the man with his tire."*

Grandpa: *"That doesn't make sense, Jarrett. Does it? By the time this angel knew there was an emergency, he couldn't drive a car fast enough from Hollywood to West Texas."*

Jarrett: *"But, Grandpa, angels work for God. God knows ahead when someone will be needing help, so he tells his angels where to go in plenty of time for them to get there. Great, isn't it?"*

That Unseen Hand on My Shoulder

Have you ever wanted to do something but an inner voice said "No"? Some outer pressure, "No," "No," "No!" Then as the events unfolded you were ever so glad for this strange prevention. Many people report they've had such experiences. And I will be forever grateful for one of mine I call "that unseen hand on my shoulder."

This is my story.

Alan and Richard were two of my best friends in junior high. They were brothers from a fine Christian home. They were good boys except, like all of us, they loved mischief. Looking back, I regret to report, some of our mischief did go too far. Stealing watermelons, tipping over outhouses, letting air out of tires, turning on water faucets, and the list goes on.

Then came the night of that unseen hand. I was sitting on our living room floor listening to a basketball game. Our university had a great team that year and I was an ardent fan.

The phone rang and it was Alan. We called each other often, especially when one of us thought up a new high jinks. And Alan's was ultra new. Altogether new. Altogether extraordinary.

Tonight we would hold up the streetcar!!!

To get the picture, you should know that a streetcar ran behind my house, less than a block away. I knew most anything you'd want to know about streetcars. I probably even knew *too much*. Such as? Such as how to disconnect the electric current and stop the car on its tracks. That bit of knowledge would be invaluable for a holdup.

Mr. McNabney was the motorman. Since this was a one-man operated streetcar, Mr. McNabney was also the conductor. A nicer man you've never met. Senior types, young folks, mothers with babies in one hand and groceries in the other, Mr. McNabney loved all, helped all. He'd never been held up. So he wouldn't be expecting us. Wear a mask, carry a gun, nothing to it. Besides, this was Friday night, pay day. We could hold up the passengers, too. Big deal. Big money. Sure thing.

But then came the unseen hand. I can feel it yet. A strong hand, solid hand, firm hand bearing down hard on my shoulder. Pressing hard. Pressing so powerfully I couldn't get up. And with it came a voice, a clear voice from deep inside me. "Tell them you're busy, Charlie. You're listening to the game. Have some more popcorn." And when that inner voice went silent, I heard myself say, "Not tonight, guys. I'm busy."

Murder is such an awesome crime, isn't it? A life is ended. No more smiles. No more, "Having a good day?" And who could ever replace Mr. McNabney? Such a terrible shock for everyone in our town. How ever could two boys from a nice home kill Mr. McNabney?

No one knew why they pulled the trigger. They didn't know. They liked Mr. McNabney too. They only knew they panicked when they realized he recognized them through their masks. How many times did I hear them say, "If only we'd come over to your house and listened to the ball game with you. Thirty years in prison? Seems like forever, doesn't it?"

The reason I heard their regrets so often was sad, too. I visited them often at the prison. Visiting hours were Sunday afternoon and the State Penitentiary was down the road, only a few miles from my college. So lonesome, Alan and Richard. They liked hearing about my football team, fraternity, classes. Except for the big mistake, they might have been at college with me. So, so sad. *And forever this will be one of my most awesome memories—except for the unseen hand on my shoulder, I might have been in prison, too.*

How many thousand times have I been over those moments in the secret chamber where I do business with the angels? Why did I feel that heavy hand pressing me down, and the inner voice telling me "No. You must not go."? Was I a better teenager than Alan or Richard? No way! In some ways I know they were better than I was. Questions, questions with no clear answers. Always, forever, answers too vague to finalize. But never too vague to whisper another prayer of gratitude.

Answer me honestly now. When the bad breaks come, do you ever resort to that old familiar query, "Why me, Lord?"

If you do—or if you ever have—why not give the reverse a try? Sometime this week, this month, this year set aside moments and do the opposite inventory. Go back in your history and ask, *"Were there times I didn't get in trouble, didn't make mistakes, didn't do some foolish thing?"* Then, when you have your answers, ask yourself, *"Why didn't I?* Was it because I had more sense, more character? Or could it have been because the Lord sent a guardian angel to lead me, to guide me, to keep me from doing something foolish, something wrong?"

If you will really do this exercise earnestly, prayerfully, I can absolutely guarantee you will add this prayer of deep gratitude to your most frequently prayed prayers:

Thank you, Lord, for all those times you've sent your "No" angel to keep me from trouble.

Why Did Those Three Boys Live?

This is the story of a hurricane along the Mississippi coast many years ago. Towns were destroyed, main streets demolished, restaurants and offices gone, schools flattened, trees uprooted, boats carried out to sea, homes broken to small bits, people killed.

I heard this story countless times from a dear old lady, a member of my congregation:

"I was a right young grandmother because I married at sixteen. We had one daughter, and then my husband was killed working on an offshore rig. Well, my little girl grew up and married the nicest young man you ever saw and they gave me, can you imagine, nine grandchildren.

"Then the hurricane struck and six of my grandchildren were killed along with their parents. My only daughter and her loving husband, gone. I tell you, it was so awful I felt like asking the Lord to take me too. Only he couldn't. Someone had to care for my three grandchildren who were left. Twin boys, spared in the little stone room at the back of their house, plus their brother. He had been upstate visiting his other grandparents when the hurricane came. Three children, all needing me now more than ever.

"So though I was not in the best of health, I had to take on a responsibility I would never have chosen. You can imagine there was no time for foolishness and we would never have made it except for a little check each month from Hurricane Relief. Was I ever grateful for that.

"Such fine boys they turned out to be. You got time? I'll tell you about them. The older boy, he went to Seminary and became a Methodist minister. I am so proud of him and you'd be too if you'd heard him preach. When the Bishop appointed him to a big church upstate, he told him "No, thank you." He preferred staying right there along the coast where he thought the people might need him more. A wonderful boy, don't you think?

"Now to the twins. Both chose a big school in Florida to study weather. All kinds of weather things, like hurricanes, floods, tornadoes, and drought. They made names for themselves in that field. One wrote regular weather columns and the other ended up teaching at the university. He taught weather prediction, that's what he taught. It seems like everyone in the family has a yen for helping people.

"Such smart boys, all three of them. Finest kind of wives, wonderful children—we're talking about my great-grandchildren, now. I tell you, those "greats" do kind things for a great-grandparent. You never saw a finer lot anywhere.

"I must have asked the Lord a million times, *Why were my daughter and most of her family killed? Why did I have to raise those boys alone?* But I guess we all have unanswered prayers, and it looks like this will be one of mine till I get to heaven. I finally quit asking and told the Lord he could explain it to me when I get there. Meanwhile I just did the best I could and taught my three little tykes to live grateful. Especially I taught them to live grateful their angels got there when they did. I think people have better lives when they live grateful, don't you?"

Millicent

"Except Ye Become as Little Children . . ."

Grandpa: *"This story really puzzles me, Jarrett. Why would six children and their parents be killed in a hurricane, yet three children live? Some things just don't make sense, do they?"*

Jarrett: *"Ever since I read a book about heaven, things like this make more sense. Maybe the six brothers and sisters who were killed were the lucky ones. What if they all have neat jobs in heaven where they are doing more important things than the three boys who were left? I think it's nice the grandma was there to take care of the twins and their brother. If you look at it this way, it could have been nice for everybody, couldn't it, including the ones in heaven and the ones here on earth. I like to think of it that way, don't you?"*

Lord, may I never grow so adult
that I cannot sometimes
think like a child.

"I Went to Sleep on My Bicycle"

You've heard of people going to sleep in their cars? Well, I went to sleep on my bicycle. I'd like to tell you my story because I feel sure an angel saved my life that day.

It was early morning, like 5:00 A.M., and I should never have gone to that slumber party. Why had I gone? Because it was a good-bye party for one of my best friends. She was moving to Chicago and all us girls wanted one last good time together. That's why I was half asleep when I folded my papers at 4:00 A.M. and started my route.

I was the only girl with a paper route. Back when I was young, girls didn't have jobs like that. I was lucky because my father worked at the newspaper. My route covered several miles because the houses were scattered. Almost at the end was a big culvert and at that point I fell asleep. I hit the edge of the curb near the culvert and must have flipped over into the small stream. Fortunately, the stream was frozen hard and there was lots of snow on it. When the bike hit the ice it fell on top of me and I was knocked out. I don't know how long I was there before I was rescued. The way I was found is what made me believe in angels.

Lots of cars must have passed me carrying people to work. But no one could see me from the road. I might have stayed there a long long time, too, except for some sidewalk construction work across the street.

One of my teachers and her husband took a brisk walk every morning. They said they'd never walked over on the culvert, but this day they had to because of the roped-off sidewalk. So here they were walking by where I had fallen. My teacher told my parents and me that she just happened to lift her eyes when she noticed something red move.

We figured it must have been my red mitten and for some reason my hand happened to raise up to my head at the exact moment my teacher glanced to her right. Of course, when she saw the red they stopped to investigate what could be in the ditch. There I was. They thought I was dead. They lifted the bicycle, she called my name, and I came to. In a little while it was almost like nothing had happened to me. They knew I would be all right, so they finished their walk and I finished my route and went home. I didn't even miss school that day.

I am sixty-seven years old now and you can understand when I say this: Ever since the day I went to sleep on my bicycle I have been a strong believer in angels.

Charlotte

"Except Ye Become as Little Children . . ."

Grandpa: *"What would you tell her, Jarrett?"*

Jarrett: *"I think it had to be angels."*

Grandpa: *"Why?"*

Jarrett: *"Because so many things sound as if it was angels."*

Grandpa: *"Such as?"*

Jarrett: *"If she had fallen in the street she might have been hit by a car. Or she could have hit her head on the pavement and broken something. But when she fell in the ditch she landed on the snow. That would be a nice soft place to land, wouldn't it? And here is something else that sounds like angels. Why did she raise her hand with the red mitten at the exact moment her teacher happened to be looking that way?"*

Grandpa: "*Anything else?"*

Jarrett: "*Yeah. If you deliver papers and have to get up at four in the morning, don't go to slumber parties."*

"Angels in My Pansies"

Part Six

Lessons from the Angels

When angels step aside and let us work our own little miracles, isn't that a good thing, too?

Kevin and His Pearl-Handled Knife

My name is Kevin and I want to tell you how I prayed for an angel and one came. When my father died, my mother gave me his pearl-handled knife for my very own. That was about the nicest present anyone ever gave me because my father was my favorite person. My mom says it's an "heirloom" pocketknife because my grandpa gave it to my daddy and now it is mine. Some day if I have a son, I will probably give the knife to him.

You can see why I'm proud to show this special knife to my friends. One day I took it to school and everybody thought it was neat. I left it with some friends while I went to get my homework assignment. My friends took the knife to show to other friends, and somehow my heirloom disappeared.

Well, I was awfully upset when I returned and nobody knew where my knife was. I started asking everyone about it. Nobody knew. Somebody said, "Probably David stole it. He does that a lot, you know." But when I asked him, he said he hadn't seen it.

I had to tell my mother when I got home that afternoon. We both cried. When I told her somebody said probably David stole it, she cautioned me not to accuse David unless I was sure he had taken the knife.

This is what happened next. When I went to bed, my mother suggested I pray about my knife. She believes in angels a lot and said I should ask for an angel to tell me where to look for my knife. So I did.

I went to sleep right away, but in the middle of the night I woke up, wondering, "Could I have put the knife in my marble box?" I ran downstairs to take a look and guess what? There was my knife in with the marbles! Then I remembered. I hadn't left the knife with friends after all. Instead I had put it in my marble box for safekeeping and I hid it under the marbles. I should tell you in our school nobody steals marbles because everyone has his own supply.

Anyway, in the middle of the night I woke my mother to tell her and then I said, "How could I ever have done anything so dumb as to forget where I put my knife?" She said she's always doing stuff like that and when she does she tries to remember these words: PRAY FIRST.

Kevin

"Except Ye Become as Little Children . . ."

Jarrett: *"Grandpa, did you ever put something away and forget where you put it?"*

Grandpa: *"Sure. And do you know what? The older you get the more that happens."*

Jarrett: *"Yeah. I noticed."*

Grandpa: *"I'm sure you have, but take it from your Grandpa, when you lose something the first thing you should do is pray. I promise you if you trust the Lord and take a positive attitude, the angels are more likely to help you."*

Jarrett: *"Thanks. Good idea."*

The "Good Fear" Angel

My name is David and I will tell you a story about what happened to me at my grandmother's house last summer. I do not have a father, so my mother has to work very hard sewing clothes at the factory. In the summer I go to stay with my grandmother. She lives on a farm quite a long ways from us. She has a pony named Alice. Alice is black and white and can run very fast.

My best friend in the summer is Wallace. We met in Sunday School at my grandmother's church. He lives three miles away, so I ride Alice to see him. It is a safe road to ride because hardly anything but small trucks come on our road. This is because the bridge is old and not safe for big trucks. I love to ride fast because I like to hear the sound of Alice's hooves on the pavement and I like it most when we go across the bridge.

One day Wallace and I were playing and I forgot to leave on time. That meant I was going to be late getting home to grandmother's and she would worry. So I was riding faster than ever. All of a sudden Alice stopped and I nearly flew over her head!

She had never done that before! Nothing I did would make her move. I kicked her in the side, I switched her with my reins, I scolded her, which I hardly ever do. Finally I got off and looked around for something that might have scared her. Then I walked up to the bridge and what do you think? The bridge had fallen in! It had broken in the middle and, if Alice hadn't stopped, we might have been hurt bad. We might even have been killed is what some people said.

I put some big limbs on my side of the broken bridge to warn everyone else. Then I went back to Wallace's house and called my grandmother. She came to get me by a different road. My grandmother didn't scold me, so on the way home I asked her: "How could Alice have known the bridge had fallen in?"

Grandmother said there are special angels she calls "Good Fear" Angels. Sometimes it is a good thing to be afraid because that will keep you from dangers you should be afraid of. Sometimes, she said, being afraid like that is a gift from God. Then she told me another thing. The Good Fear Angel probably knew I wouldn't listen because I was in too big a hurry. So the Good Fear Angel told Alice to stop instead of trying to tell me.

I like that, don't you? I am glad angels really are smarter than I am and sometimes ponies are, too. That is a good thing, isn't it?

David

"Except Ye Become as Little Children . . ."

Grandpa: *"David's grandma talked about the 'Good Fear' Angel. That's a new term to me, Jarrett. What do you think it means?"*

Jarrett: *"I think it means there are some things we should be afraid of. And angels can help to tell us what they are."*

Grandpa: *"Can you give me an example?"*

Jarrett: *"Sure. In gymnastics there are certain things you should be afraid to do because if you tried them you would get hurt bad. Or you should be afraid to cross the street with a car coming. Or you should be afraid to hit your sister. Everyone should be afraid of some things. Even grandpas, they should be afraid of grandmas sometimes, shouldn't they?"*

"Angels in My Pansies"

When I was little I was crazy about pansies. Because of that, one spring my mother took me to the store and we bought all kinds of pansy seeds. Then she showed me how to plant them and let me do it all by myself. I planted them in front of our house, and I wish you could have seen them when they bloomed. They were every color you could imagine and I was so proud. But then the weeds came and pretty soon you could hardly see the pansies anymore through so many weeds. So I said something to my mother about the weeds and she told me since I planted the garden I had to pull the weeds. Only I didn't do it for a long time and they just got worse.

Finally my father said he wouldn't stand for it any longer because the front of our house looked so terrible and he was going to pull up everything, including my pansies. Of course I cried, so my parents told me I had until Monday to get the weeds pulled or the next week the weeds with the pansies would all be gone.

Well, I got to work. It took me all day that Saturday, but finally I finished and was I ever tired. But you should have seen my pansies. They were bigger than ever, more beautiful than ever, and my parents said they were proud of me.

Well, in our Junior High Class at Sunday School we had been learning about angels. Maybe it's why that very Saturday night I had this dream. In my dream some angels were out in my pansies picking the prettiest ones. I asked them what they were doing. They told me they were picking a bouquet to take back to God because he thought pansies looked like angels. That made me so happy all I could do was cry.

At breakfast I told my mother and father about my dream and do you know what my mother said? She said, "See what a wonderful thing you did? The angels didn't come until *after* you worked all day pulling those weeds. That's how angels do it, Susan. They want you to do your part and then they will do theirs."

I have thought about this ever since it happened and that really is how it works. You know what I mean? It seems you can't wait around for other people a lot of times. You have to begin yourself before good things come to you.

For instance, there was this girl in our class who always bothered me. I didn't like her at all, and neither did anyone else. It was really gross the way she acted. But I thought about my pansies again. I began trying to do nice things for her, treating her special, and can you believe this? She doesn't seem like the same person. Now she is one of my best friends and a lot of people like her. I asked mother if she thought some angels changed her. Mom said probably so, but they had to wait until I did my part.

I learned all these things from my pansies. Every year now I plant more pansies. And if you study the faces on pansies, they really do look like angels, don't they?

Susan

"Except Ye Become as Little Children . . ."

Grandpa: "*What's the big lesson here, Jarrett?*"

Jarrett: "*I think it's the word my parents keep telling me: RESPONSIBILITY. And sometimes I don't like it any better than what's-her-name.*"

Grandpa: "*Her name is Susan.*"

Jarrett: "*OK, Susan. There are some things angels won't do for Susan or for anybody, no matter who they are. You have to do those things yourself. I guess the angels sit around and see if you're going to be responsible enough to start working. Then, if they see you're working, they may come and help you.*"

Angels on His Rearview Mirror

My Uncle Clyde was a trucker. He drove an eighteen-wheeler and I often got to go with him. If you were riding in Uncle Clyde's big truck you would see a wooden angel hanging from his rearview mirror.

Uncle Clyde was a hobby woodworker. When he wasn't driving his "rig" (that's what he called it) you would find him out in his shop making all sorts of neat things. He made tables and different kinds of furniture. He even made a playhouse for my sister and me. It was beautiful, and all my friends wished Uncle Clyde was their uncle. But he also did something else I want to tell you about.

Uncle Clyde made angels like the one hanging from his rearview mirror. It was made of wood and he said it didn't make any difference what kind of wood you used. If the wood wasn't pretty he could paint it and make it look real nice.

I know you will want to know what he did with his angels. What he did was to give them away. Mostly, he gave them to other truckers. He said some of them were religious and went to church like he does. But he also said some of them never went inside a church. Some truckers even did things that were not nice, but they still wanted one of his angels. One thing I liked especially about my Uncle Clyde was that he would give his angels to people like that. He hoped his angels would make them want to be better.

Stuart

"Except Ye Become as Little Children . . ."

Grandpa: *"Where do you suppose Uncle Clyde learned about angels?"*

Jarrett: *"I bet they had a Bible in the home where he grew up and maybe they read it together. Maybe he was in an accident himself one time and an angel came to him, so he wanted everybody to get acquainted with angels. One way he could do that was to make angels in his shop and give them away. I like the part where he gave the angels to the good people and the ones who weren't so good. I think it's important to be nice to the people who aren't so nice, and that's hard sometimes, but Jesus did it, didn't he?"*

Three Angels in a Cemetery

We lived in a small town, a great place to grow up. It was so safe we could go almost anywhere and not be afraid. We even walked through the cemetery on our way to school. You asked for people to write to you about angels, so I am but these are a different kind.

In the cemetery was a gravestone with three concrete angels on top. Before we knew the reason for those angels my friends and I wondered about them. We would often stop and try to figure out why anyone would want a tombstone like that.

Then one day our teacher gave us an unusual assignment. At the library we had to read in a certain book about the history of our town, then write a report about a piece of history we had discovered in our reading. For the most part, our reports were very boring.

But this one girl in our class decided to find some answers about that grave marker. Why were those angels on that tombstone? Whoever thought that grave marker up? Well, she found the answer.

Many years ago a terrible fire burned a family's house to the ground. The fire began at night and started at the back of the house where three children slept. That part of the house was burned almost before anyone knew the house was even on fire. As a result, all three children died in the blaze. Their grieving parents put an angel for each child lost in the fire on their own tombstone.

It's really a sad story, isn't it? But I think what's more interesting than sad is what else our classmate found. She discovered in her reading there was an inscription on the grave marker. None of us had ever seen it because the whole area was overgrown with weeds. The inscription must have been hidden from view for years and years.

Being curious, we got the necessary tools and cleaned it up to see what it said. We made it a class project, so many of us pulled weeds, cut briars, and rubbed away dirt. Finally we got to the inscription and this is what it said:

Aren't You Glad You're Alive?

Nathan

Do you have room for one more interesting hobby? All my life I've had a fascination with what's written on grave markers. (I call it Charlie's cemetery collection.) Some are pensive, others provocative. Many are solemn, but a few of them are humorous. My favorite? On a small country church tombstone someone had carved the poem:

As you are now
So once was I.
As I am now
You soon will be.
Prepare to die
And follow me.

Somber, for sure. But some wag had scratched under the heavy verse:

To follow you I'm not content
Until I know which way you went.

The Cat That Walked Twenty-Two Miles

Part Seven

Angels and the Animals

One Brown Swiss calf lonely for her mother; one small kitten on a long, long journey. Large dog guiding lost girl to her own back door; two simple wags of a tail. Is there a special contingent of angels who do their thing with animals?

Every one of us who has ever had a favorite pet would say, "Of course!"

"Halo," the Brown Swiss Calf

When I was a boy, I had a Brown Swiss calf named Halo. She was a beautiful animal. Twice she won first place at our state fair. She won when she was a yearling calf and again when she was a grown milk cow. But she didn't get off to a champion's start.

Halo's real mother died when Halo was born. My father and I kept Halo alive by feeding her with a bottle, but she didn't do well. We knew she probably wouldn't make it with hand feeding, so my father put this ad with our phone number in our county paper.

> WANTED: Nursing cow for hungry calf. Mother died at birth. Fine stock. Son's 4-H project. Willing to pay well. Please call if you can help.

We were very sad because no one answered our ad and Halo was getting weaker. We all knew it wouldn't be much longer. Then, ten days after the ad came out, our phone rang. It was a Mrs. Noble. She was a little old lady who lived in a town thirty miles from us. (We thought her name was just right for the kind of lady she was.)

Mrs. Noble hadn't read her papers because she was in the hospital. But her neighbors had saved them for her. So now, just home from the hospital, she was reading everything to occupy her time. That's why she had seen our ad. So she called and asked would we please come over?

Of course, we went to her house right away. Sure enough, she had a Jersey cow that had birthed twin calves, but they had both died. Her cow was almost overflowing with good Jersey milk. And can you believe this? Mrs. Noble said she wouldn't take a cent for us to use her cow! Why not? Because her son and daughter had been in 4-H when they were my age. Well, with all that rich milk Halo began getting better right away and grew into the state champion. The first year Halo won we went home to get Mrs. Noble and bring her to the fair. We wanted her to see Halo with the blue ribbon. Mrs. Noble was so happy she cried.

I forgot to tell you I named my calf Halo because I think angels were watching out for her. Don't you?

Adam

"Except Ye Become as Little Children . . ."

Grandpa: *"Do you think angels care about cows, Jarrett?"*

Jarrett: *"Of course they do. They work for God and we know God loves animals."*

Grandpa: *"How do we know that?"*

Jarrett: *"Well, he made the animals even before he made Adam and Eve. That's in one of the Bible books I read. I also read about Noah and how God saved two of every kind of animal. That means he saved a lot more animals than he saved people on that ark!*

"I like that part about how a poor little calf was saved. It makes me think of Boswell, our cat. You know how big and healthy he is. Well, when we got him he was the poorest in his litter. He just stood there waiting and hoping for us to take him. When I see him now, I wonder if an angel didn't tell us to take him for our cat."

The Cat That Walked Twenty-Two Miles

I am going to tell you a story about Jennifer. She is our cat and we have had her a long time. She had a baby kitten named "Trip," and I will explain why we named him that.

My father works for a computer company and, because he is very smart, he has a big office and tells everybody what to do. When I was twelve, he was transferred to a town named Buffalo. He didn't really want to leave my mother and me, even for a little while, but somebody had to sell our house so my mother and I stayed here. Ours is a very nice house but it cost a lot of money so we didn't know how long it would be before somebody bought it.

Then about one month later somebody wanted to buy our house, but you can't guess what happened. That very week my father called up from Buffalo and said we should keep our house. He was suddenly being transferred back here because the man who was head over a whole lot of plants and offices had a heart attack and died. My father called to say he would be taking this man's place here. That meant he would be even more important than he was going to be in Buffalo.

My mom and I were so happy we didn't have to move because we loved our house and had lots of friends. My grandparents live here, too. We were so glad. The first night Dad came home we all ate supper together to celebrate. After dinner we joined hands and prayed together to thank God all this happened.

We hold hands and pray around the circle every day. If your turn comes and you don't have something to say then you can squeeze the next person's hand so they say their prayer right away and pass you. This night everyone prayed.

Now I will tell you about Jennifer. She is a grey-and-white cat with pretty long hair. When we thought we were going to move to Buffalo, we gave Jennifer to my cousin and her family. They live in another town twenty-two miles north of us. Our family felt very bad about giving Jennifer away, but we couldn't have a cat in our new condo.

When the news came we wouldn't be moving I said I wanted Jennifer back. But Mother told me it wouldn't be fair to my cousins. Then we found out Jennifer was going to have babies! So then my mother said maybe we could have one of Jennifer's kittens. And that was very exciting.

My aunt called when Jennifer had her kittens and we went over to see them.

She'd had three, but two were weak and died. I loved the one left and could hardly wait till it became mine. Then my aunt phoned to say Jennifer had disappeared with her kitten!

Now I am going to tell you something I suppose you can hardly believe, only it truly happened to us and we couldn't hardly believe it either. We were holding hands after supper when all of a sudden right in the middle of our prayer we heard a cat meow. It came from our back porch and it sounded exactly like Jennifer. Of course, we all ran outside to see and there she was! But that isn't all. *She had her baby kitten with her.* Then when we picked Jennifer up to pet her she wanted down and do you know what she did? She took her baby kitten in her mouth and went around to each of us, showing off her new baby. It was so beautiful we all cried.

You can imagine how happy we felt. We just couldn't believe Jennifer could be back with us. "How did she get here?" we wondered. Did my cousins bring her and leave her at our house? But we knew that wouldn't have happened because they would have stayed for supper. So my mother called her sister and she was so surprised and so glad that they both cried some more.

My father said he'd heard of cats making long trips back home. Then he said, "I guess when we all said good-bye to Jennifer, Jennifer never said good-bye to us." But how could she manage to walk that far and carry her baby too?

My father called the newspaper and a reporter came to interview us and take pictures of Jennifer and her baby. My father asked them to have anyone who could have seen our cat on her trip to please phone us. Three people called and said Jennifer came to their house with her baby and they had fed her. But she wouldn't stay and at night she disappeared. Another person phoned to say he had seen a cat going over the big bridge across the lake. That bridge takes quite a while for even a car to go over.

We studied maps, and this is what we found. In order to get from my cousin's to here, Jennifer had to cross a lot of roads, including three freeways. She also needed to go through two towns, plus all those miles of farms and some hills too. It all seems so impossible but here she is and now you can see why we named the baby cat "Trip."

One day our minister asked my father and me to tell our cat story in church. We took the animals in a cat carrier and I even got to come up by the pulpit and hold them for everyone to see. My father said angels must have been guiding our cat home with her baby and protecting them on their trip. When he finished the story the whole congregation stood and clapped and some of them cried. Then our pastor said sometimes in the Bible God worked through animals and birds and even fish. And of course he used angels. I think that is a good thing to know, don't you?

Lucinda

The Big Brown Dog

My name is Gretchen and I will tell you a story about what happened to me when I was six years old. We lived in Vermont because my father had a job with the park service. There was a big forest behind our house. My parents told me real often never to go into the woods. I really didn't need to because my father made lots of things for me to play on right there in our back yard. He built these things in his shop.

One day a black squirrel came in our yard. I had never seen a black squirrel so when he ran into the woods I followed. He didn't go very fast, like he wanted me to follow him. So I went wherever he went and pretty soon I was lost. Then when I turned to walk back, it seemed like every way I went the woods just got thicker and thicker. Finally, I came to a clearing and sat down on a stump. I put my face in my hands and cried and prayed.

All of a sudden I felt something licking my face. I was almost scared to open my eyes, but I did. What do you think it was? I will tell you. It was a big brown-and-white dog. He was huge, the biggest dog I'd ever seen. Later my father said he must have been a Saint Bernard.

Anyway, he stopped licking my face and started pulling on my skirt. I knew he wanted me to go with him so I did. You may not believe this, but after a long time he brought me to my very own back porch. I ran into the kitchen and my parents were so glad to see me they didn't even scold me. So we all ran outside to see my new friend, but he was gone. We called and called and looked all over, but he wasn't anywhere around. We live in a very little town so my parents asked everybody if they had seen a big brown dog around. And guess what? Nobody had seen him or knew anyone around there who had a dog like that either. Everyone in town talked about it a lot. Some people also said he was probably a Saint Bernard, but one lady said she thought he was an angel dressed like a Saint Bernard.

My parents are religious people so naturally I asked if he was an angel. My mother said no, but an angel must have sent him. She said if a real angel came to me out there in the woods, I might have been too scared. But if an angel sent a nice dog to lead me home, I would like that. Well, I sure did like it and all my life I will believe in angels. I also think they can do anything they want to help a person. Thank you.

Gretchen

"Except Ye Become as Little Children . . ."

Grandpa: *"This story puzzles me, Jarrett. No one in the town had ever seen the brown-and-white dog. Where did he come from?"*

Jarrett: *"Probably a Saint Bernard kennel was some place close and the angel knew he could borrow a dog there. Maybe he had borrowed dogs there before. Like this may even have been a special loaner dog, one the angels borrow all the time."*

Grandpa: *"Sounds kind of complicated to me, Jarrett."*

Jarrett: *"Yeah, but angels know how to uncomplicate things real fast. They'd have to know that, wouldn't they?"*

Chester Wagged His Tail Twice

Almost killed by a car, Chester was nearly lifeless when they reached the veterinarian's office. Agnes Ann, his little mistress, begged both the doctor and her parents not to put him away. "Let him live at least overnight. That way when I say my prayers I can ask God to send an angel to make him well again. We've been studying about angels in school [she attends a parochial school] so I think I know how to pray for an angel's help. Please, please."

The next morning Chester still looked lifeless. But what was this? When Agnes Ann called his name, Chester wagged his tail twice.

"Well, that was a long time ago, Dr. Shedd, and you should see Chester now. He is more beautiful than before and his pretty black coat is shinier than ever. Oh, sure, he still limps a little, but what if I hadn't prayed for an angel? I think he is still alive because I did that, don't you?"

Agnes Ann

"Except Ye Become as Little Children . . ."

Grandpa: *"What do you think of Agnes Ann's question? So what if she hadn't prayed for an angel? Would Chester have lived anyway?"*

Jarrett: *"Maybe. But didn't God tell us we should pray about everything? And that has to mean pets, too."*

The Bible says:

In *everything* by prayer and supplication
with thanksgiving let your requests
be made known to God.
Philippians 4:6, RSV

"All I Remember Is the Twenty-Third Psalm"

Part Eight

Traffic Ways for the Angels

Lord,
Week after week,
Year after year,
Help me to be some angel's helper
Somewhere, some way.
And give me what it takes to stay with it.

Amen

Was Miss Fanchon Really an Angel?

One day a little boy knocked at the teacher's front door. She was retired, and her name was Miss Fanchon. She had never been married so everyone called her an "old maid." She was fussy about some things, but I had been watching her and decided she might be the person I needed.

So here I was at her door saying, "I know a little boy who needs someone to love him. Do you need a little boy like that at your house?" I will never forget her answer. She said, "I most certainly do. Come in, Charlie." She made me some hot chocolate and gave me some just-baked cookies.

After that she introduced me to her new canary, then told me the names of every fish in her aquarium. She got out her scrapbook and showed me her family. Then she found pictures of the classes she had taught, all thirty of them. She said she could still call every student by name, and I am sure she could. Over and over she told me all of her classes were not really classes at all. Every one was a collection of interesting individuals, each person very important.

That's what I needed to hear right then. I have never forgotten her. And I have tried never to forget her lesson that day, plus the many others she taught me over her still-warm cookies and hot chocolate.

It's been seventy years since I knocked at her door to ask if she needed a little boy. I still remember her welcome smile. And for all the years yet coming to me, I will forever thank God for the caring love she gave me.

Was Miss Fanchon really an angel? I certainly thought so at the time. But she would probably have been the last to say she was an angel. Yet Miss Fanchon will always be one of the angel's true helpers to this hurting child with his hopeful query, "Do you need a little boy to love?"

"Except Ye Become as Little Children . . ."

Grandpa: *"What do you say, Jarrett?"*

Jarrett: *"I think an angel must have told her you were coming because she had hot chocolate and cookies ready for you. Maybe she was one of the angels' regular helpers. Don't you think if she never married she needed a friend, too? It seems like people who are angels' helpers get helped by being angels' helpers."*

The Doctor and His Golden Retrievers

He was a neurosurgeon who raised golden retrievers. You couldn't buy one of his dogs. He gave them away. Now why would he do that? This is his story.

"When I was a boy just about the age to begin school, my mother sent me to the store one winter day. Winter was my favorite season. I especially liked it if the snowplows hadn't come out yet. Snow to play in, ice to slide on, friends together outside.

"We lived in a small New England town where everyone knew everyone else. It was perfectly safe for children to be out by themselves. All the people were friendly, all the animals were friendly, including my neighbor's dog. His name was Napoleon and he went with me everywhere.

"This particular day it was extra snowy and very cold. The walks were terribly slippery, but that made going to the store even more fun for Napoleon and me. Everything went fine until I came out of the grocery. As I started across the street a teenage driver came roaring out of the alley. He was going much too fast and headed straight at me. His windshield was frosted over so I don't think he even saw me. But there were people waiting for the bus. They saw it all and they told my folks I would have been killed if it hadn't been for Napoleon. When he saw the car bearing down on me, he hit me square in the chest, knocking me back up on the sidewalk. Napoleon was a golden retriever.

"My wife and I are both doctors, and what do you suppose we do for a hobby? We raise dogs, special dogs, golden retrievers. We have three females and a champion male named Napoleon II. I love my dogs, not only because of the memory of the first Napoleon. I love my dogs because of what they're doing today.

"Golden retrievers are naturally gentle animals, but we teach ours to be what we call 'extra-gentle care dogs.' They love people in nursing homes, retirement centers, and children's hospitals. After we've trained them, we give them away to places like this. We've never sold a single dog, although people would pay well for them because they're all blue ribbon winners.

"You said you would like to hear from people with angel stories, so I thought I should write. My mother was convinced it had to be an angel who directed

Napoleon to save my life. To this day I believe she was right. You can understand then how much satisfaction I get out of raising my golden retrievers to help the angels help other people."

Bruce

"Except Ye Become as Little Children . . ."

Grandpa: *"This is one of my favorite stories, Jarrett. You know how much I like dogs. And I sure like what the doctor is doing with his golden retrievers. They are blessing so many people and all because Napoleon I acted so fast when Bruce was a little boy. He says some people saw what happened. There must have been others around, so why do you think an angel would use a dog to save a boy?"*

Jarrett: *"I think it was because dogs can move faster than people. The adults would have had to discuss it and maybe appoint a committee. And someone had to move fast to save him. Dogs don't have to stand around and discuss things. They just DO IT!"*

Grandpa: *"Do you remember the grandma who told about the 'Good Fear' Angels? Do you suppose there are 'Fast Love' Angels, too?"*

Jarrett: *"Sure, why not?"*

Mrs. Kaltenbach Helped the Bread Angel

If you had tasted even one bite of Mrs. Kaltenbach's bread you would say, "*Nobody* bakes bread like Mrs. Kaltenbach bakes bread."

She was a member of the church where I grew up as a boy and all of us in the church knew what she was doing. The Kaltenbachs didn't have much money; her husband Emil worked in the refinery as a clean-up man. But every week she baked twenty loaves of her bread, put them in her apron, and carried them across the tracks to the poor. She always had a way of knowing who needed them most.

The people across the tracks were the poorest of our town. Some of them had been born there. Others drifted in when their luck went bad. Still others were recent immigrants who barely spoke English, but Mrs. Kaltenbach could manage that too. She and Emil had come from Germany themselves, so she knew how it felt to be a stranger in a strange land. Across the tracks was tough terrain. It was all there: crime, drinking, gambling, fighting, shooting, everything.

I was in Mrs. Kaltenbach's Sunday School class and she was one great teacher. We called her "Miss K" and somehow it fit her exactly. She was a fascinating personality, with that brogue and broken English. We loved her, she loved us, and it was one super love-in.

The adult members loved "Miss K" too; they didn't want her going across the tracks week after week. "Too, too dangerous. One of these days they'll mug you, rob you, hurt you, maybe kill you. Please don't go anymore. Why don't you sell your bread to the restaurants and coffee shops? You could make a whole lot of money, enough to build a new home. Take it easy, you deserve it."

Then she would smile and tell her story again. When she and Emil were new to our country they lived in New York City. They lived where the poor lived because they were poor. Once each week a knock came at their door. It was a lady giving away German bread. Right then, she and Emil decided if they ever had the chance they'd like to help the hungry like that lady did. "I tell you true," she would say. "She was like an angel."

Minus the brogue, I could almost recite the rest of her story:

We never knew who the lady was in New York City. Sometimes we asked her name but she would say she couldn't stay. She must knock on the next door. So for twenty years I've been going across the tracks with my apron full of loaves.

In all those years no one has ever hurt me. No one has been unkind. No one has tried to rob me. They call me "The Bread Angel" but I tell them, "Please, you have it wrong. Call me 'The Lady Who Helps the Bread Angel'." And if you look for it, boys and girls, there will be some way you can help an angel, too.

Like I said, I was only a boy of six or seven, maybe eight.

But wasn't it absolutely great to sit week after week under Miss K and hear her teach? Then to watch her go week after week across the tracks with her apron full of bread loaves, that was great too. Impressive. So impressive I've never forgotten and never will. My guess is that every student who ever sat under her teaching, every one of us who watched her deliver her bread, as long as we live we'll still be praying:

Lord,
Week after week, Year after year,
Help me to be some angel's helper
Somewhere, some way.
And give me what it takes to stay with it. *Amen*

"All I Remember Is the Twenty-Third Psalm"

This is a story about Psalm 23 and what happened one summer in a hospital room. I know it happened exactly like I'm telling you because I was there. Like many pastors, I am big on the Shepherd's Psalm. I use it often in my pastoral visits.

This time the patient was a high school boy badly hurt by a freak accident. Daniel was standing with his father at the mill. They were grinding corn. Suddenly a bolt came loose and flew across the platform. It struck Daniel in his temple and down he went. For three months Daniel lay in a coma. Consciousness zero. Communication zero. Hope almost zero, too. But his parents, devout people, stubbornly held to the faith that someday he would wake from the darkness. And they were right.

Three months and six days after the accident, Daniel sat up and said, "I want to go home."

It's a beautiful story, isn't it? And for me it will always be one of the most meaningful memories of my ministry. Why? Because at least once each week I stood by Daniel's bed, held his hand, and said Psalm 23. Daniel and I knew each other well. I often refereed basketball games where he played.

Then came the day of his miraculous recovery. Naturally, after Daniel's return to consciousness, his parents asked, "Do you remember anything from those months in your coma?"

"All I remember is the Twenty-Third Psalm," he answered. "I remember saying it over and over, lots of times, with someone."

Amazing, isn't it? Not once did he open his mouth those three months. Not once did he appear to know what was going on. Not once did he speak a single word. But there in his darkness, he heard it all, understood it all, spoke it all. And I've often wondered what was going on in those inner chambers of his unconscious mind when we recited this mighty phrase:

Yea, though I walk
Through the valley
Of the shadow of death
I will fear no evil
For thou art with me.

"Except Ye Become as Little Children . . ."

Grandpa: *"Amazing story, isn't it, Jarrett?"*

Jarrett: *"Do you know whether he knew the Twenty-Third Psalm before the accident?"*

Grandpa: *"No, I don't know. But do you suppose he could have learned it by my having said it so often?"*

Jarrett: *"Maybe, but I just thought of something. I wonder if angels can talk to people when they are unconscious. If they do, maybe an angel taught him, because he knew you'd be coming to say it with him."*

The Bible says:

"So shall my word be that goes forth from my mouth;
it shall not return to me empty, but it shall accomplish
that which I purpose, and prosper in the thing
for which I sent it."

Isaiah 55:11, RSV

Gunther and Gisela Get Their Baby

Among our friends, my wife and I are known as the "German G's." That's because my name is Gunther and hers is Gisela. Our parents both came from Germany. Both our fathers were farmers named Rudolph, and both died within a year of each other. I am now running both the family farms.

Gisela and I have always had an extra strong marriage. The first five years were happy except in this one area: We had no children. Although we tried everything, it was no babies for us. Finally the doctors said we'd never have any. That's when our troubles began to get serious. Gisela wanted to adopt, but no one in our family had ever adopted. I was the one holding back. I guess I was ashamed or maybe a little afraid. Yet I knew Gisela was very sad.

One day we were at the state capital for a football game. I'd been on the team when I was in agriculture school. Gisela graduated in home economics from the university, too. We never missed a game.

That particular day we won the big game and we were way up. So we celebrated by going to dinner with friends. Strange, isn't it? That restaurant is directly across the street from the Child Refuge Center, a placement agency of our church. When we said our good-byes to our friends and were ready to go, Gisela looked at me. "Please," she said, "can we go see the babies?" Of course I wanted to please her, so we went.

Then came the first surprise. Greeting us at the door was Beatrice, a classmate of ours from the university. She had been a close friend of ours at school, but we hadn't seen her since graduation. You can imagine we had a great visit. She asked about our family and we told her everything, including our lack of children. Beatrice asked why we didn't adopt and Gisela got tears in her eyes. It was an awkward moment because I couldn't think of any adequate reasons for my hesitation. Of course we made no official application that day, but Beatrice did say she'd call when a nice baby came.

On the way home we were both very quiet, but that night before we went to sleep Gisela put her arms around me and said, "Gunther, going to the Refuge Center was the nicest thing you have ever done for me. Thank you." That time she didn't say anything about adopting a baby and I didn't either.

Now comes the part I can hardly believe. Almost four months later Beatrice called to say a newborn boy was at the refuge. He had already been named Rudolph since he came from a German couple, but of course adoptive parents could change the name if they wanted to. Rudolph! Just like our fathers! Was this a sign?

Well, you can imagine what happened. That very week we went to the city, signed an official application, and began the process to make Rudolph our first child. We were so pleased, we adopted three more in the next ten years.

It's been over thirty years now, thirty wonderful years. Each of our children has finished the university. Two of our boys have completed medical school and are well into their practices. The third son farms with me and our daughter is married to a farmer. They live just a few miles from us. But all this is still not the best part. We are grandparents four times over and another grandchild is on the way.

Sometimes in the evening Gisela and I sit reminiscing about our love and our family. We wonder about how it all came to be. Gisela with her beautiful simple faith is absolutely sure our family is the work of some special angels. I wish I could be as sure as she is. What do you think, Dr. Shedd? Can you help me?

Gunther

"Except Ye Become as Little Children . . ."

Grandpa: *"Gunther is having a hard time believing in angels, isn't he? And he's asking me to help him. Any ideas?"*

Jarrett: *"Sure. You could tell him all the places in his story where it almost had to be angels. Why did they go to that restaurant right across from the children's home? Why did their good friend open the door that night when she was hardly ever there at night? And didn't it almost have to be angels who named the baby Rudolph? Who else would know that both grandfathers were named that? Also, it must have been an angel who made Gunther change his mind."*

Grandpa: *"So you think it was several angels doing this job?"*

Jarrett: *"Oh, sure. I think angels work together on the hardest cases."*

"Take My Hand, Grandpa"

Can you imagine a grandfather so blessed? On Thursday evening, I go for dinner with Jarrett, Anna, and Sarah. Jarrett is eight, Anna six, Sarah three.

If you are a grandparent, you know what kind of evening that would be. If you're not, I wish for you some such heavenly experience before your earthly days are over.

On a recent evening, dinner finished, Jarrett asked, "Grandpa, would you take me to see 'Jurassic Park'?"

"But I thought you weren't allowed to see that movie until you're ten. Isn't that what your parents told me?"

"Oh, yes, but that was before I read them the book. I checked it out at the library, and after they heard it all they said it didn't sound all that bad, so my daddy took me. He liked it but I loved it and I want to see it again. I thought it would be fun if you would take me. They show it every Saturday afternoon at the Dollar Theater, right across from my favorite ice cream parlor."

So off we went, Jarrett and I. 2:30 P.M., popcorn in hand, we were there.

Before I tell you about the show, you should know what happened Friday night.

Nine o'clock the telephone rang. Jarrett.

"Grandpa, I've been thinking and I'm worried. This is a scary show we are going to see and I think, what if you are afraid? But I have it figured out what we can do. I have decided when you are afraid you can reach over and take my hand. Then you won't need to be afraid anymore."

Six times during the show, Jarrett leaned over to whisper, "This is a scary part coming up, Grandpa. You better take my hand."

Six times I took his hand and I assure you, not once was I afraid.

If you have read my *Brush of an Angel's Wing,* you will know that hands and the angels have always had special meaning for me.

- I was saved from drowning by a mysterious hand lifting me for a breath of fresh air.
- A mysterious hand on my car keys called me to the home of a poor bleeding man.
- In "The Heavy Hand on My Shoulder" you've heard my report of the firm hand which saved me from a lifetime calamity.

Were those really the hands of an angel? And if they weren't, what *do* you think they were?

Now on to one more question:

Will I ever forget that afternoon at "Jurassic Park" when a caring little grandson took my hand to allay his grandpa's fears?

No, somewhere down the millions of eternity's years Jarrett and I will sit eating ice cream and talk about that one. Isn't it awesome how an angel can reach out through a little child's hand and say, "This is your special angel whispering. You don't need to be afraid. God loves you. Take my hand. It's *his* hand!"

A Final Word from Jarrett

Grandpa: *"Jarrett, I have a question. Why is it that you children seem to know so much more about angels than the adult world?"*

Jarrett: *"That's simple, Grandpa. You adults are always going blah-blah-blah, but us kids don't do that. So we have more time to know the angels."*

The Bible says:

"Except ye… become as little children,
ye shall not enter the kingdom of heaven."
Matthew 18:3, KJV